If You Can't Be First, You Must Be Better!

A Business Plan Workbook

Phil Sigler

ISBN: 0615568734
ISBN-13:978-0615568737

DEDICATION

To Karl Parker, a friend and companion during the trials of our lives
and the test of our faith – another story we'll soon tell.

Phil wanted to teach business; Karl wanted to learn business.
Karl needed a teacher, Phil wanted a student. So Phil taught,
while Karl learned that *If You Can't Be First You Must Be Better.*

ACKNOWLEDGMENTS

To my family, friends, customers, venders, and employees (past and present) who assisted me in the creation of this book of business. Through shared experiences (good and bad), I am thankful for them all.

To my best friend, Lan along with our two daughters Kaylin & Larissa who lived without me while I wrote and taught these principles of business. I look forward to making up for all the lost time.

A special thanks goes to Karl Parker who initially encouraged me to write this book. I am grateful to my twin brother, Tom Sigler, and older brother, Dr. Tim Sigler. Thank you both for your encouragement, love, and guidance through the darkest of hours.

Mom, Dad, Grandma, Aunts, Uncles, Cousins…you are all blessings to me, I appreciate and love each of you dearly.

James Knight, Jerry Key, Michael Adams, Pastor Rick, and partners of my business – thank you for the continued loyal support you have shown.

To all the editors who proofread this manuscript, including my mother Vickie Sigler; Bernice Sigler (sister-in-law); Marchelle Fias of Brown Mackie College; and Sean Andreas (a dedicated employee)
Of course, any remaining errors are the responsibility of the author.

PREFACE

This book will reflect on the trials, struggles, and the necessary determination of successfully commencing and operating a business.

- **Reading this book will educate you in the business field**

- **Completing the workbook portion will provide a business plan**

Combined together (book + workbook) will provide a step-by-step guide in becoming an entrepreneur of success.

Topics discussed throughout this workbook include choosing a commodity to sell, financing, and the marketing of a business. This book goes into the details of a real-life company example using the PS 12/24 Principles & Philosophies of creating and running a successful business.

This workbook will inspire interest in new ideas, provide instructions for starting a business, and offer an interactive web-based business plan. With purchase of this workbook, access to the www.ps1224.com website is available to print your own business plan. With an interactive website you will have the availability to easily create, modify, and keep your business plan up-to-date.

The goal is to get your business up and running while keeping you entertained, interested, and informed through:
PS 12/24 the
12 Principles for creating a business plan &
24 Philosophies of running a successful business!

TABLE OF CONTENTS

Introduction

12 Principles of Business

These 12 principles are the steps required to create a business plan

The PS 24 Business Philosophies

Philosophy #1: If you can't be first, you must be better

Philosophy# 2: Your first investment is never money – it's always time

Philosophy #3: Whether it's money or planning - be conservative

Philosophy #4: A brilliant idea does not equal success

Philosophy #5: Present the image of success

Philosophy #6: The one who knows the market knows how to win

Philosophy #7: Pick your market strategy

Philosophy #8: A business does not have to be brick & mortar – it can be virtual

Philosophy #9: Business must outpace a building to ensure profitability

Philosophy #10: Pay as you go

Philosophy #11: Never have 50/50 partnerships

Philosophy #12: A precise and concise marketing plan is mandatory

Philosophy #13: Never add an employee who doesn't pay for themselves

Philosophy #14: Track ROI (return on investment)

Philosophy #15: Don't fear opposition – let the competition fear you

Philosophy #16: Inefficiency wastes money

Philosophy #17: Let technology replace unproductive manpower

Philosophy #18: Evaluate strategies often

Philosophy #19: Every footstep entails a price

Philosophy #20: Wearing multiple hats saves money and space

Philosophy #21: Reporting is vital to maximize profits

Philosophy #22: If business is not innovating, it could be dying

Philosophy #23: Written processes & procedures provide rest for the future

Philosophy #24: The power of persistence is priceless

These 24 philosophies are concepts for running a great business

The 12 principles are the steps required to create a business plan.
The 24 philosophies are concepts for running a great business.
Together they create the PS 12/24 Principles & Philosophies of business.

How it worked for me

The following is a true story of how I lived from the beginning to the burgeoning of a corporation so simple in concept, yet so rich in success, its story merits telling to all who wish to achieve the same.

Conceived from a trivia type question posed by a co-worker, my business materialized from an idea to an entity named SR-Systems Incorporated.

I was employed at a company based in Boise, Idaho working as a technical support agent. One afternoon a man paused at my desk holding a magazine. "Do you know internet sales will exceed a trillion dollars by Y2K?"

A Trillion Dollars! I registered little to nothing visibly, but there was an instant subcutaneous reaction. My mind raced with the dawning of a new idea. This projection in connection with the instrument used daily to perform my job 'a computer', seemed incredible and made me pause to think. This meant through internet sales…an excess of one trillion dollars would exchange hands within the next year, providing tremendous opportunity for anyone knowledgeable and prepared in the process of online sales.

Didn't someone say, "We've come a long way, baby?" Well, technologically speaking we have. In 1998, transacting an online sale needed a device known as a 'modem.' For money to hit the market in the form of an online sale – every computer connecting a shopper to the World-Wide-Web required a modem.

Principle #1:
Identify A Need

Between the money and the market laid a modem. Why not market the device a trillion dollars must pass through in order to meet the demand of an online purchase?

> *Philosophy #1:*
> *If you can't be first,*
> *you must be better.*

I only had to find a way of getting these devices to people faster and better than others. Considering the concept of capitalism, 'supply and demand', principle met the present with the realization there was a market 'demand' for modems; a need for which I could find the 'supply'.

Principle #2:
Locate A Supply

Everything I knew about business – admittedly not much at this time – posed the idea that I needed two things to get started: First a product to supply and second a partner who could help develop an ecommerce website. I shared my passion for business with my co-worker and he was equally full of optimism and entrepreneurial energy.

> *Philosophy #2: Your first*
> *investment is never money*
> *– It's always time.*

Principle #3:
Formulate A Plan

We began running numbers and working countless hours to formulate a business plan. Visualizing high profits with multiple retail stores, our fantasizing was left unsupported.   It was decided to be realistic and conservative; not only on our spending but also in our planning.

> *Philosophy #3:*
> *Whether it's money or planning*
> *– be conservative*

The next step in our business plan was to discover a business name.   We decided upon a business name that left an opening for future expansion called SR-Systems (SRS). We had a great idea and now needed to make sure it would actually work before spending a dime.

> *Philosophy #4:*
> *A brilliant idea does*
> *not equal success*

A considerable amount of time was consumed deciding the look and feel we wanted our aspiring company to represent. It was decided to have an appearance of a major distributor thriving with preparation and success. At SRS we presented an image not according to what we were, but what we wanted to become. This would be accomplished by listing a plethora of products on a website, providing an image of a warehouse with inventory ready to be sold and shipped.

> *Philosophy #5:*
> *Present the image of success*

Principle #4:
Research Market Statistics

Set ablaze with the impetus of a new idea, much effort was poured into research. We began researching market segments and found resellers in need of a supplier for modems. In addition to our research, rigorous testing was required to determine which manufacturer had the highest quality modem at the lowest possible cost.

> *Philosophy #6:*
> *The one who knows the market*
> *-knows how to win*

Principle #5:
Know Your Strategy

The competition was selling modems at $25.00 each. After a series of negotiations and a $2,500 PO (Purchase Order), our cost became $15.00 per modem. This price allowed our business strategy to be set as a low price leader.

> *Philosophy #7:*
> *Pick your*
> *market strategy*

After three months of web development and the arrival of our modem shipment, SR-Systems was now in business with an ecommerce computer hardware World-Wide-Website, www.srsystems.com

> *Philosophy #8:*
> *A business does not have to be*
> *brick and mortar*
> *– it can be virtual*

This website allowed our business to be operated from my home. The garage was our warehouse; the bonus

> *Philosophy #9:*
> *Business must outpace a*
> *building to ensure profitability*

room was the sales office. Our strategy was keeping our costs low – not buying anything we didn't need, and even what we needed we waited until the operation demanded it.

> *Philosophy #10:*
> *Pay as you go*

Principle #6:
Set the Proper Infrastructure

At this moment we had identified the need, located the supply, created a business plan, performed research, and set strategies into action; it was now time to set the proper infrastructure of the business. It was agreed, I would be president of the corporation with a 55% ownership and my friend the vice president at 45%. My investment was $5k while his equaled time, energy, and dedication into

> *Philosophy #11:*
> *Never have*
> *50/50 partnerships*

building our website. I made the capital investment and he made the labor investment.

Principle #7:
Meet the Demand

With the company infrastructure set, money in hand, our website ready to launch, and modems in stock; we were now ready to meet the demand through marketing.

> *Philosophy #12:*
> *A precise and concise*
> *marketing plan is mandatory*

Within a month of precise marketing our newly developed e-commerce website made its first sale. An individual in Buffalo, New York, purchased a single modem for $23.50. We were excited to see our business in action.

Principle #8:
Prepare Attitude
and Aptitude

Our first sale – Our first lesson: I recall amusedly, is not one you'd wish to pattern. Fortunately for us, our first lesson was during our initial transaction. With an $8.00 shipping fee from Boise to Buffalo, $1.00 in merchant services (credit card processing fees), and .50 cents for packaging material – our profit was negative $1.00. We did not factor shipping costs or the plausibility of selling a single modem to one individual. Taking encouragement from the words of Henry Ford, "Failure is the opportunity to begin again more intelligently," we knew in future sales to factor the "soft costs" of business.

Behind the scenes of an operation appearing to buzz, more orders began rolling in. Determined not to lose sales by projecting an image of inexperience, it was decided to hire help for the increased sales volume. The candidate chosen was a previous

> *Philosophy #13:*
> *Never add an employee who*
> *doesn't pay for themselves*

co-worker who consistently received awards for his quality of excellence in customer service. He accepted our offer and within 20 minutes he proved his worth. He picked up the next call uttering a script like a pro, "Thank you for calling SR-Systems Incorporated, how may I direct your call?" Sounding to the caller as though they were placed on hold; he would simply pass the cordless phone so we could assist them. Just by changing the way we answered the phone, existing customers began commenting we had grown into a huge call center overnight. To torture a cliché, the sky really becomes the limit when all members of the business play for the team.

We began an advertising campaign vastly marketing in newspapers, radio, TV, billboards, and bus benches.

> *Philosophy #14:*
> *Track ROI*
> *(Return on Investment)*

Recognizing the high costs in advertising, we realized that tracking these expenditures was crucial.

As sales began to increase so did the competition. The solution was to

> *Philosophy #15:*
> *Don't fear opposition – let the competition fear you*

offer something new and better. We located a manufacturer in Taiwan that sold chassis of various shapes and colors. At that time in history the computer market only offered a standard beige computer case. This was our opportunity to offer the public something new and exciting. After contracting with the Taiwanese, SRS became their Western U.S. distributor. Presenting customers with this option dramatically increased our computer sales and before long our technicians were customizing computers in many colors, shapes, specs, and sizes. Adding modifications to these chassis and accessorizing them with see-through-window kits, florescent lighting, and LED case fans, created a new fad that caught on rapidly and became known as "case mods".

Principle #9:
Focus on Efficiency

Daily shipments from FedEx, UPS, and even semi-truck loads required us to locate a warehouse as we outgrew the confinement of my home. While obtaining a warehouse to lease we also looked for ways to save money through efficiency. Every credit card sale had to be keyed in manually and all web orders had to be entered into an accounting database. This job process became so demanding that it

> *Philosophy #16:*
> *Inefficiency wastes money*

required a full-time employee dedicated to entering these transactions. During our search for efficiency we located a new technology in credit card processing, allowing online transactions to be integrated into our database and processed automatically. This change in technology dramatically

Philosophy #17: Let technology replace unproductive manpower

increased the productivity and efficiency of doing business.

The new costs of a warehouse facility created the urge to recoup the added expenses of a building. The solution arrived by offering computer repair services. Affordable pricing was our theme and we continued this model by providing a $50.00 flat fee computer repair service. This low rate service charge brought an additional revenue of $10k per month.

Philosophy #18: Evaluate Strategies Often

By our fifth year of business expansion began with the opening of two retail stores named, "Computer Central". This name told people exactly what we sold, whereas SR-Systems left questions in consumer's minds. I recall a neighboring store owner driving across town to one of our retail stores named Computer Central. They were not aware SR-Systems sold and repaired computers. By changing the name, there was no doubt – we were in the computer business.

Principle #10:
Implement Reporting

In order to have efficiency and maintain growth, accurate reporting was essential in maximizing our profits. The requirement arose to hire a financial controller to watch the cash flow and provide weekly reports. As sales grew, so did our overhead. With new sales representatives it was interesting to see how each employee changed the cost of doing business. The utilities,

Philosophy #19: Every footstep entails a price

insurance, and supplies drastically increased. To ensure every employee was efficient as possible we gave every worker multiple job functions to help save costs. Our controller was the HR (human resource) manager, the warehouse supervisor was also the RMA (return merchandise

Philosophy #20:
Wearing multiple hats
-saves money & space

agreement) representative, I handled the purchasing and sales while my partner handled technical support and marketing.

Principle #11:
Ensure Appropriate Financing

Philosophy #21:
Reporting is Vital to Maximize Profits

By year ten the company reached $6 million in sales with the release of our new brand of computers called "*Force*". These systems were sold into the SLED (state, local, and education) space. With the increase in sales for the *Force computers,* new relationships were needed for financing. We met with bankers and carefully chose a financial institute that would help us in our continued growth. We also increased our corporation's net assets by purchasing our own building instead of leasing.

Philosophy #22:
If business is not innovating
– it could be dying

Principle #12:
Plan An Exit Strategy

With the concept of "location, location, location" in mind, I partnered with my Uncle Jesse from San Pedro, California to purchase a two acre parcel of land on the corner of a busy intersection. This two acre parcel left room for our computer store and future expansion. The building was constructed with the latest advancements of technical support equipment and custom shelving. With the image in mind to potentially model this store for future locations, we spared little in creating the representation of a high end computer store. The look portrayed a high class appearance but a low price feeling. Our service sales rapidly increased and nearly doubled by year end.

computer *central*
powered by *Systems*

Envisioning the future, our next growth segment may involve franchising. With developed processes and written procedures it allows the company to carry on without missing a beat.

> *Philosophy #23:*
> *Written Processes & procedures provide rest for the future*

Looking back, nothing was easy and hard work was required to ensure its success. Everyone was determined and focused to see the business become a great success story. This accomplishment came from never giving up. When brick walls blocked our vision we found ways around them, over them, under them, and sometimes even through the brick walls in order to achieve our goals.

> *Philosophy #24:*
> *The Power of persistence is priceless*

With this introduction of "how it worked for me" completed; let's begin the necessary PS 12/24 Principles & Philosophies of business, so you can see "how it can work for you".

<u>How it can work for You</u>

(Philosophy #1: If you can't be first, you must be better)

Being first to market is always best. If you can be the first to market a new conceptual idea or skill, you are ahead in the game. New ideas create their own atmosphere of excitement, influencing people to be the first to try something new. Manufacturing companies often fight to be the first to introduce the latest technology. Competitive corporations take risks of releasing a product early just to ensure they are known as the first. Being first receives all the buzz, PR (public relations), and the recognition.

I witnessed a manufacturer release a new product to the industry early to outpace the competition. The manufacturer received a huge increase of technical support calls due to the lack of QC (quality control). The corporation increased temporary staff for a month to provide solutions to their customers. The company weighed these extra costs and made the decision that being first to market was worth the added costs.

The point is; if you can invent a new product, offer a new skill, or provide a new service that is unique and first of its kind - it is always best!

So what if you're not offering something new?
The answer is the second part of philosophy #1...You simply, **"do it better!"** There are many companies that compete by offering something better or by providing a better service. For instance, Yahoo came out in 1994 and offered a good web surfing interface. Three years later in 1997 Google offered customers a cleaner and faster search engine. Google is now worth ~$190 billion versus Yahoo at ~$35 billion.

MySpace had a brilliant idea which they offered first to the market but then two years later Facebook came and offered something similar but better. Facebook is now the most visited website in the World. Neither Google nor Facebook were first to market their service but they did offer something that most people liked better. This leads us into our first chapter of identifying a need or a want that others may desire.

Principle #1: Identify a Need

A true entrepreneur can be successful no matter where they are in the world. They seek out opportunities in the environment to empower success by discovering a need others may have or want.

So let's imagine for a moment you have been transported and left stranded on an island. The island inhabitants are struggling to survive with no available employment. A true entrepreneur would quickly determine a commodity that everyone desires and turn that, into the new currency. Since water surrounds the island the easiest possibility of creating a new currency could be selling fish. Food can be a potential currency as everyone needs it. Other islanders may already be catching fish using poles. So your challenge would be discovering a more efficient method of harvesting fish.

In the example above we can identify the first and second phases of being an entrepreneur:

Phase One – **Identify a need**
Phase Two – **Find a way to do it better**

The need is food and the product chosen is fish, now how can you improve the process? A few options may involve using nets, a wooden raft, or different bait; these options allow you to catch a variety or an abundance of fish allowing your fish to be the best offering on the island. The point is…it doesn't matter if you are selling fish, computer parts, or anything else. You can rise above the competition by following the *PS 12/24 Principles & Philosophies of business.*

The goal is to get you motivated in locating a need or a want which you can provide to others in a better fashion.

A startup business I assisted desired to compete in the computer gaming industry. They would setup computers and gaming consoles for consumers to play computer games. Their only competition was a company called the "Gaming Center". The first step in competing is to find a way to do what?..."**Do it better**". Projecting an image of something bigger or better than the Gaming Center begins with the *'name'*. I explained they should call themselves the "Gaming Arena". The name of a company helps deliver the message that you want to portray to the public. The Gaming Arena sounds more valiant and like a place where people will come to compete. When consumers hear a name of a business they begin sizing it up, deciding which business deserves their hard earned money. If one wanted to compete in this industry they could call themselves the "Gaming Universe". Both the Gaming Arena and Gaming Universe sound bigger and better. The name of your business can attract consumers to your door first.

Better in some cases is faster.....................Ferrari, Porsche, Corvette
Better in some cases is simplicity.................Google vs. Yahoo
Better in some cases is cheaper..................Dollar Store or Walmart
Better in some cases is more convenient.......McDonalds, Subway, Walgreens
Better in some cases is more variety............Restaurant Buffet, Baskin Robins
Better in some cases is high quality..............Snap-On Tools, BMW, Mercedes
Better in some cases is better service............Craftsman lifetime warranty
Better in some cases is simply....................JUST BEING BETTER.

Now that "Better" is on your mind, think of things you can do better than others. The goal for this first chapter is to invent, offer, produce, or create a "need" or a want that is worth selling to others. Take time to write the skills or talents that you may do better than the competition.
(Be honest and realistic with your traits.)

1. _____
2. _____
3. _____

Have you identified a need, a want, or a service that you can offer to others? _____ (yes / no)

Is this offering a product or a service? _____

Will you be First to Market something new? _____ (yes/no)

Are you doing something better? _____ (yes/no)

What makes your business distinct, unique, or better? _____
_____

What is your strongest selling point?
_____
_____

What is the exact need, want, or desire you are trying to fulfill?_____
_____

Is there a real need for the product / service in today's market? _____
Explain:_____
_____

Why will the business be successful?
_____
_____

Would you buy/use it yourself?_____ Would you sell it to a friend?_____

Are you excited about this product / service? _____ Why?_____
_____

Can you imagine yourself selling this item for the next several years?_____

What are some potential names for your new business? _____
_____   _____   _____

    The reason for these questions is to ensure that you believe in the product, if not then you probably won't be successful at selling it. Find a product or service that meets both the needs of others and your own ability to locate, purchase, and resell it.

Principle #2: Locate A Supply

You may have the best idea in the world however, there must be a supply and a way of getting it to the public. Numerous people have expressed their business ideas and for some I can quickly determine that obtaining a supply would be extremely difficult or even impractical. Personally, a lint free dryer sounds cool but how realistic is it? The idea of being lint free is convenient, but investing money into this creation may not be a good investment as the concept may be infeasible to accomplish. The product or solution you provide must be obtainable and realistic. There are many inventions each day and some are quite impressive and even overwhelming in belief. We must keep a realistic perspective and know how to obtain the supply. Keep the product offering simple in the beginning and then expand when the time is right.

Provide a description of the product or service: _____
_____

Where will you obtain the supply? _____

Are there other suppliers? _____ Who are they? _____
_____ _____ _____
(Have you considered what will happen if the only supplier you have chosen files bankruptcy, a natural disaster occurs, or their building goes up in flames?)

You have to expect the unexpected and plan ahead for the worse case scenarios. When a major hurricane hit Taiwan, computer hard drive prices tripled and left a major shortage in the market for a solid three months. If a business is not prepared it can make a short sprint for longevity.

Knowing the resources available will prepare you for locating suppliers and verifying a need. Which resources are available to you?

	Networking:	Internet Searches:	Books/Articles:
Name/ Business:_____	_____	_____
Name/ Business:_____	_____	_____
Name/ Business:_____	_____	_____

Principle #3: Formulate A Plan

Once a product or service has been chosen to sell, it is time to set a foundation for the business. This construction begins with a business plan which takes effort.

(Philosophy #2: Your first investment is never money – but is always time)

You must take time to initiate planning. Careful planning is a major means of improving output to obtain the results you anticipate. The business plan begins with a basic overview and slowly becomes more in-depth on various facets of the business.

A business plan is like a resume of your experiences and the opportunity to prove your business on paper. On a personal resume you list your career objective, experiences, skills, employment history, education, achievements, and references. Much like a personal resume, a business plan entails very similar traits. It is the chance to show potential investors, customers, employees, vendors, and bankers your expertise. A business plan includes all the necessary steps to drive the company forward with clear goals for everyone involved. That's why this book is focused on detailed planning and helping you consider the possibilities one can encounter in business. A business plan will keep everyone focus driven and on target to achieve the same goals.

Mistakes in startup businesses primarily consist of two things. The first is improper planning – People rush through their business plan instead of spending the time needed to obtain the foresight or predictions of the ups and downs that may occur. You must thoroughly plan and develop goals before starting out. As Ben Franklin said, *"If you fail to plan – you plan to fail"*.

With that said, planning for a business seems to never go as planned. If you plan to have a business running in three months you should anticipate six. One of our stores took nearly nine months before opening while another took only four. Construction, TI's (Tenant Improvements), and permits can cause huge delays along with other unknowns.

The second mistake often made is improper funding. Determine the "capital" (money) needed to begin your business. Many startup companies are undercapitalized and they are doomed before they even begin. Companies can grow too slowly creating a lack of funds to pay the overhead costs, or they can grow too quickly and not be able to sustain the business. In either scenario the result is the same -> the business collapses due to the lack of funding. *"Prior proper planning prevents pitiful poor performance"*.

If one plans a budget based on a three month time frame for cash to flow and it takes six months, then the business will struggle to make up the deficit. This lack of income throws the whole financial business plan out of whack. Being conservative is of the utmost importance; conservative not only with money but also in planning.

(Philosophy #3: Whether it is money or planning - be conservative)

An example of a business model that showed a high potential for profit was one I invested in called, "Playa De Rosarito" located in Mexico. It was a fantastic concept of building a hotel and selling the suites as timeshares. The land was located on a beach in Rosarito. It was required to have a Mexican corporation and a U.S. corporation in order to purchase this land. I invested $50k as a silent partner along with seven other VC's (Venture Capitalist = investors).
The business idea was to build an eight story hotel with 17

suites costing roughly $3M. Each suite would sell for $25k allotting the owner to have a one week stay each year. When doing the math of 52 weeks in a year ($25k per suite times 17) the outcome is ~$22M (52 x $25,000.^{00} x 17 = $22,100,000.^{00}) a very nice return for each VC.

(Philosophy #4: A brilliant idea does not equal success)

On the negative side the three main owners of the business began traveling to and from Mexico spending money foolishly. They only looked at the big payout and not their expenditures. Within the first year they had spent all of the investor's money. The end result was seeing the company go defunct, filing bankruptcy and my investment wasted. This lesson is to make it clear…don't become blinded by an idea.

Start small; test the waters, don't spend money unless needed. My corporation was ran out of my home until I had no other alternative. I never leased equipment or spent a dollar that I didn't have to. I believe in operating a business and living way beneath my means. I drove a '94 Nissan pickup for ten years while most of the employees drove newer vehicles. I waited until I could pay cash for the vehicle I wanted and then purchased it.

While remembering these two mistakes in business (**improper planning** and **inappropriate financing**) be sure to think conservatively as we work through the creation of your business plan.

To begin, set the vision for your company. The vision statement of a business plan is a general statement of the facts you can offer. The overview needs to be clear to you, clear to co-workers, and clear to the customer.

A friend recently asked for help with creating a business plan for a hookah bar. I will use that company as an example to answer the next series of questions for your own business plan. We wrote an explanation on how he would strategically enter the market and created a statement of purpose for his business.

Vision Statement: Selling a variety of hookah flavors, hookah accessories, and entertainment. The company will provide shish tobacco in various flavors along with music and dancing.

What is your overview / vision statement?

_____
_____
_____

With your Vision Statement completed we can get a little more specific. In the hookah bar scenario we discussed entertainment and accessories being offered. The products available for purchase included: Hookah shish, coils, hoses, bowls, stems, and mouth pieces. The service / entertainment offered would be: Live music, dancing, finger foods, non-alcoholic drinks, glow sticks, and karaoke.

What are the products and accessories you plan to sell?

_____
_____
_____

Will there be accessories or complimentary products you can add?

_____
_____
_____

In today's economy it is essential to offer some type of service. Services help maintain relationships with customers. In addition, there is a greater profit margin to be made. Mathematical equations prove, businesses that offer services grow exponentially faster by retaining more profits than businesses that don't.

What will you provide as a service to your customers?

_____
_____
_____

By looking for Re-occurring Revenue Streams (RRS) or Consumer Replaceable Parts (CRP) you can increase sales and contacts with your customer. Examples of these include:

1. Monthly service <u>contracts</u>:
   (Subscriptions, membership dues, Web hosting, etc.)
2. Annual, Quarterly, or Monthly <u>maintenance</u>
   (Oil changes, haircuts, tanning, checkups, network monitoring)
3. Consumer Replaceable Parts (<u>CRP</u>)
   (Toner, batteries, tires, etc.) –Printer manufacturers make more money on their CRP, the "ink," than the actual printer.
4. <u>RRS</u> (Re-occurring Revenue Stream) and add-on items that compliment the product being sold.
   (Expansion packs, upgrades, add-on parts, etc.)

Recently I purchased a Braun shaving razor with a self-cleaning bay. The bay requires a cleaning solution cartridge which lasts about 2 months before needing replaced. Each time I purchase a new one I am reminded of a perfect example of an add-on item. Not only does Braun make money on the initial sale of the razor but now they make money on the cleaning cartridges for the entire time I have this razor. It is an excellent example of a reoccurring sales revenue which wasn't previously in their product line. A consumable item that needs replaced on a regular basis is one way a retailer can establish long term sales.

By establishing a customer base with contracts, maintenance, CRP's, and RRS's customers will have continual contact with your business and potentially buy more from you. These underlined items keep your business in the mind of the consumer.

Are there contracts, maintenances, CRP's, or RRS's that can be offered? _____ If yes, list them: _____

_____

_____

Don't forget, service or reoccurring revenues are great places to focus.

Next, add more detail to your offering. In the Hookah bar scenario it would be listing the exact flavors being sold. After researching the top selling flavors in the industry we listed: berries, vanilla, orange cream, cappuccino, Red Bull, and pink lemonade. Then we listed the most popular music people would want to hear while smoking hookah.

List more details of your offerings: _____

_____

_____

While helping this friend establish a business plan and seeing all the wild entertainment he wanted to provide to his customers; I asked if the business name chosen matched the offerings. It appeared to me that the name chosen was not portraying the image he was describing to me. I suggested calling this new business "Hookah Loco", this name not only tells what the business is selling but also portrays an image of a crazy fun place to hang out. The public perception, however conceived, must be one of preparation and success.

(Philosophy #5: Present the image of success)

There should be no guess work involving your business name. Establish a name that communicates to customers exactly what you are selling. As mentioned earlier, SR-Systems didn't explain the most essential part of our business, "computers," thus the creation of Computer Central. This new DBA (Doing Business As) did justice and increased the sales for our retail division.

Designing your business name can be as easy as using your last name or something that is meaningful to you. However, that name may not help in the marketing efforts of the business. Before purchasing the business name, spending resources on developing a logo, paying for business cards, and developing a website – make sure you are committed to the name chosen. In addition, perform research and make sure the name chosen will be a good choice for many years to come.

Referring to page 13 does your business name match what you are selling? _____ (The business name should be short, memorable, easy to spell, easy to pronounce, and original.)

Can you change or come up with a better name? _____

You can search the business name from the U.S. Patent and Trademark Office (USPTO) or by going to the secretary of state website to verify availability. http://www.uspto.gov
Have you researched your business name to make sure no one else has it? _____

Is your business name available?_____

What is the name of your business?_____

The final step of planning is to write a mission statement. A mission statement tells others what you want to accomplish. The mission statement for Computer Central is:

At Computer Central we provide customers the latest and greatest computer technology at the lowest possible prices. We are forever testing, educating, and proving to be on the cutting edge of technology in this fast-paced forever changing technological world of electronics. When you need to buy a new computer, fix your old computer, or build your own computer; Computer Central is readily available with all the items you need in stock and will offer the very best customer service in the industry.

Your mission statement should be bold and identify your offerings to the customer. It is your final sales pitch of why they should come to you versus the competition.

What is your Mission Statement to the consumer?_____

_____

_____

_____

_____

_____

_____

_____

How will you accomplish this mission?_____

_____

_____

_____

Notes:_____

_____

_____

_____

_____

_____

_____

Principle #4: Research Market Statistics

(Philosophy #6: The one who knows the market – knows how to win)

According to *Webster's New Explorers Thesaurus* - Research is the act or instance of *seeking truth*, *information*, or *knowledge* about something. This is exactly what one must do when starting a business. The more research you conduct will either support your business plan or make it clear that it may lead to a potential downfall.

'*Seek truth*' of the product you're selling or offering. Check the quality and the performance thoroughly. Put it to the test and validate every dimension of it. Once you have proven that everything lives up to the expectations promised, then begin moving forward. Personally, I can only sell products that I truly believe in. I know our computers are fully tested and have been proven over and over again. I feel confident offering a 3 year warranty due to the high quality of products we sell and the technicians we employ.

Gather as much '*information*' as possible on the *product*, the *market segment*, the *demographics,* and your *target audience [defined later]*. Researching the **product** entails investigating where the product is made, what material(s) were used, the pros/cons, quality of the product, longevity of the vendor, and the stability of the manufacturer. Researching information about your business is what it takes to become better than the competition.

When looking at the **market segment**, determine if your target audience will be consumer retail sales, government (Gov.), education (EDU), business to business (B2B), SMB (Small Medium Business), health care, or enterprise level businesses. Market segmentation is the process of dividing each customer into groups based on their purchasing behavior. Categorizing customers by similar needs or characteristics will help you in providing the proper advertising to meet your customer's demands.

Commonly examined marketing **demographic profiles** include *gender, age, employment status, education, income level*, and *population* in the region. These demographic profiles are necessary for you to know in order to sell your product wisely. Researching the population of customers in your area helps provide an idea of how many potential customers are available for your offering. Find out how many people live in the surrounding area and how many of those people would be buyers of your product.

Concentrate your marketing efforts on a six mile radius from your location and the following six miles of customers will automatically come. Then focus the next wave of advertising on an 18-24 mile radius. The word of mouth, advertising exposure, and buzz generated will engulf the extra six miles of consumers. Don't have a broad approach when it comes to advertising or you will be just shooting in the dark and missing your prime opportunities of clientele. Be focused and concentrate on the customers at your back door first.

When asking business owners who their target audience entails, too often the response is "everyone". Realistically that is never the case. A **target audience** is a specific group of people within a market segment you should be aiming towards in your advertising. There are many factors to be considered including various lifestyles, cultural differences, age groups, and fads. In addition, times of the day and days of the week are factors to consider. There will be different times through-out the day where peaks in sales occur, plateau, and taper off. Is your target audience going to be kid friendly and will that bring more people in or turn them away? There are numerous scenarios to consider.

Having in-depth knowledge on the four topics we discussed (*product, market segment, demographics, and target audience*) will give you a clearer picture on the proper channels of advertising. This information will provide a greater idea of the clientele that are suitable to your target market.

'Knowledge' - Know your products, limits, and strengths better than anyone else. Most importantly, focus on the strengths and make sure there is a market for your product. Some people have the "American Idol Business Syndrome" where they think they have a great business idea but reality proves differently. Similar to the auditions on American Idol where people believe they are America's top singer; many striving entrepreneurs think they have a successful business model but it is only going to set them up for failure. An example of a poor business model I witnessed was a lollipop store. It opened in a new fancy constructed building near a Wal-Mart super store.   The lease on the building had to be atrocious and would probably take selling 10,000 lollipops just to pay the rent. To make matters worse, the product offering was very similar to the variety one could buy at Wal-Mart at the fraction of the price. Remember the old saying, "Where's the beef?" I instantly thought to myself "Where's the market research?"

Nothing worthwhile ever comes easy. Invest time into knowing the most you can about the market segment you are getting involved in. As Hamilton Holt stated, "Half effort does not produce half results, it produces no results." Therefore, **learn everything you can about the business before you begin**. Seek the truth of the product being sold so you can possess the knowledge needed to run a business successfully.

Is this a seasonal business? _____

Which seasons do best? _____ _____ _____

Who is the manufacturer of your product? _____

Who are the suppliers? _____ _____ _____
How long have they been in business? _____

Where is the product made? _____

What type of material is used to produce the product?_____

What are the top 4 products being sold / used?

_____ _____ _____ _____

How financially stable are these manufacturers from 1 – 10?____ ____ ____ ____

Who is your market segment? _____

Which age groups are you targeting? _____

Who is your target audience? _____

What is the radius in miles of the targeted customers? _____

What is the population in that radius? _____

How many people would be interested in the product? _____

How many customers do you expect?:

_____   _____   _____   _____   _____
6am-10am   11am-3pm   4pm-8pm   9pm-1am   2am-5am

What percent of these customers will buy something? _____%

What is the average selling price? $_____

Describe the product knowledge and include how you obtained it:

_____

What is your competitive edge in the market place?

_____

_____

List the Pros and Cons of the product and or service:

Pros: _____

Cons:_____

Principle #5: Know Your Strategy

This workbook provides help in creating a plan, but you have to supply the effort and must strategize against the competition. Strategy is a more in-depth word for "planning" which is to arrange, realize, and achieve something. The key word is to "achieve" by winning over the consumer and… **doing better** than the competition.

In every business there are <u>strengths</u> and <u>weaknesses</u>; correspondingly there are <u>threats</u> and <u>opportunities</u>. It is your job to know each of these. Possessing average strengths will not set you apart from the competition. You must be far better in your offering, knowledge, and strategy than the opposition. Distinguishing yourself from others is how this is accomplished.

When reviewing <u>strengths</u> begin looking at what you are offering and why a consumer would be purchasing from you over the competition. To determine your business approach, focus on a few of the following:

Price, Quality, Performance, Speed, Variety, or Service.

(Philosophy #7: Pick your market strategy)

No one can do it all; review the list and see where your energy should be focused. A corporation may switch gears between these 6 choices but only 2 or 3 should be focused upon at one time.

When SRS sold products based on price we didn't have time or resources to offer a high quality customer service. Some customers who purchased a motherboard $5.00 above cost, would also expect our sales team to help with the installation. These few consumers could not grasp that our company sold on price and not service. The point is, a company cannot survive selling products at a low cost margin and provide high quality of service. Our retail stores on the other hand are purely service oriented and each sales rep is well trained and educated in answering technical questions. The items sold at Computer Central have a 20% margin with their market strategy based upon service where SRS is based on price. You simply can't do both! The strengths from one company is very different from the other, however both companies are successful at what they do.

Which of the six Market Strategies will you focus on?

1._____ 2._____ 3._____

(Price, Quality, Performance, Speed, Variety, or Service)

How will you accomplish these strategies?_____

_____

_____

_____

_____

_____

The three market strategies not listed above are your <u>Weaknesses</u>. There is no way to offer all six market strategies a consumer may desire. The competitors may offer low prices; possibly higher quality solutions, faster performance, and quicker delivery...whichever the competition possesses you must find solutions to do it better or have a different market strategy to focus upon. A competitor may beat a price on a product we sell but their customer service cannot compare to the personal attention and knowledgeable staff provide at Computer Central.

List the top 3 competitor's market strategies:

_____ _____ _____

Competitor # 1　　　　　Competitor # 2　　　　　Competitor # 3

When considering <u>threats</u> be sure to know what they are before you begin. Analyze the competition and consider future competition. You must know your limits and the amount of funds "money" that is available. Don't get financially in debt trying to compete on "variety" while accruing a surplus of inventory. Don't compete on similar solutions if you're not guaranteed to do it better. Remember that the competition can be evolving and adapting as well. Look at the $5.00 sub sandwich market. I believe Subway came out with it first, and now nearly every sub sandwich place offers a $5.00 foot-long sandwich to compete. That $5.00 marketing idea caught on rapidly and everyone began to mimic it. Same with the dollar value meals that so many fast food joints now offer.

List the top 5 competitors: _____ _____

_____ _____ _____

What are their strengths? _____ _____

_____ _____ _____

In miles what is their distance to your business?

_____miles, _____miles _____miles _____miles _____miles

Do any of these competitors sell the same product line? _____

What are the top selling items of the competition? _____

_____ _____ _____

What is the competition's selling price on the top 5 competing items?

$_____ $_____ $_____ $_____ $_____

What are the top 4 threats or disasters that could affect your business?

_____ _____ _____ _____

The last and most important strategy is to know the opportunities available to you. Creating your own niche in the market will separate your business from the competition. Opportunities lie in places where the competition isn't focused. If a competitor is selling on price – focus on better service, higher quality, or faster performance. The competition may have huge loans and be gravely in debt with building costs, old inventory, and uncollectable debts; while you can begin competing more intelligently. There could be considerable advancements in technology over the competition or different methods of selling products through online sales from the confinement of your own home resulting in huge savings.

(Philosophy #8: A business does not have to be brick & mortar - it can be virtual)

Small businesses often feel the need to have a building in order to spur initial growth, but I suggest working from your home when possible before spending unnecessary finances. Businesses fail when they have more building than they have business. There are many successful business owners who have an EBay store or an ecommerce website as their destination, versus a building. Craigslist, Yahoo Store, or other marketing websites might be the perfect choice for you.

(Philosophy #9: Business must outpace a building to ensure profitability)

The façade of a small business operation is not necessary; what you don't have during the first phase of business doesn't matter as much as what you do have. Working from your home can allow you to invest in more sales reps versus the overhead of a building. Many business owners would love the opportunity to start fresh with the current knowledge they possess, but overwhelming day to day tasks and debts prevent that from happening. One of your greatest opportunities of beginning a business is to begin with controlling your debt. Now is the prime opportunity to never waste money, and only buy when you absolutely have to.

(Philosophy #10: Pay as you go)

You have the opportunity of being creative and can research all strategies of the competition, distinguish their strengths, recognize their weaknesses, identify their market strategies, and formulate the best opportunities in the market before spending a dime.

What opportunities can you list? _____ _____
_____ _____ _____

What is your niche in the market?_____
_____
_____
_____

Have you tested your product to see if it will sell to family members, friends, co-workers? _____ Would they buy / use your product?_____
                                        (if no….maybe reconsider)

How are you distinguishing yourself from others? _____
_____
_____
_____
_____

Principle #6: Set the Proper Infrastructure

With the plan set, research performed, and the strategy in place it is now time to work on the infrastructure of your business. The infrastructure of a business includes obtaining the business <u>name</u>, the <u>type</u> of business you should have, and the <u>chain of command</u> in your organization chart (Org Chart).

Obtaining a business <u>name</u> begins with creating a DBA (Doing Business As) or filing corporate papers with the state that you are conducting your business in. A DBA can also be referred to as an Assumed Business Name, Trade Name, or even a Fictitious Name. The purpose behind a DBA is to prevent two local businesses from operating under the same name. However, a DBA does not protect a company from any legal rights to the name as a Trademark does. A Trademark is designated by the following symbols:

TM (Unregistered trade mark)

SM (Unregistered service mark, used to promote or brand services)

® (Registered trademark)

There are 4 common choices in selecting a <u>type</u> of business organization:

1. Sole Proprietorship (1040c Schedule)
2. Partnerships (1056)
    a. Limited Liability Partnership (LLP)
    b. Limited Liability Company (LLC)
3. Non-Profit Organization (990)
4. Corporation (1120 or 1120s)
    a. S-Corp
    b. C-Corp

Determining the type of business to create depends on the size of your company, sales revenue, and members involved. Listed below is a clearer description for the type of business organization to choose from.

Sole Proprietorship:
one needs a business license from the city, a DBA, and a business checking account. A Sole Proprietorship is a type of business entity that is owned and operated by one individual with no legal distinction between the owner's personal assets and the business. The owner accepts full responsibility of everything and owns all the debts and assets of the business. This is the easiest way to go when beginning a small business adventure and to test the waters of a home-based business. You can obtain a Sole Proprietorship by simply getting a business license from your local city.

Partnership:
is accomplished through a Limited Liability Company (LLC) or a Limited Liability Partnership (LLP). For this type of business you will need to apply for one of these licenses through the Secretary of State office. Often times an attorney or CPA (Certified Public Accountant) is recommended to create these types of companies. A LLC or LLP is a flexible blend of a corporation and a partnership which protects the owners from their personal assets being attached to the company. It is a limited protection but is more protective than a Sole Proprietorship.

Non-Profit Organization:
are corporations formed for a charitable, civic, or artistic purpose. Nonprofits are generally exempt from federal and state taxation on their income, and so they are often called "exempt organizations." Nonprofits have substantial responsibilities for reporting their activities, income, and assets to ensure that they are in compliance with federal and state laws governing charities.

Corporations
provide a high level of security against personal assets. A corporation is a completely separate entity and even receives its own Tax ID number (Employer ID) which is similar to a social security number. An Employer ID is used in place of a partner's social security number and allows the business to act as its own identity. States require about a $200 filing fee for the company to become incorporated and will issue a "certificate of incorporation" upon completion. There are two classes of corporations to choose from. There is an S-Corp and a C-Corp and the differences are: Shareholders of a corporation may elect to treat the corporation as a flow-through entity known as an S corporation. An S corporation is not itself subject to income tax; rather, shareholders of the S corporation are subject to tax on their pro rata shares of income based on their shareholdings.[1] To qualify to make the S corporation election, the corporation's shares must be held by resident or citizen individuals or certain qualifying trusts. Unlike corporations treated as S corporations, a corporation may qualify as a C corporation without regard to any limit on the number of shareholders, foreign or domestic. Bylaws and two officers are required.

Knowing the different types of business organizations – which type best fits your business?_____
(Sole Proprietor, Partnership, Non-Profit, or Corporation)

The Organization Chart or chain of command is important to set in the very beginning when partners or investors are involved. You have to pick one person who ultimately will be in charge and is responsible for solving any disputed concerns within the corporation.

(Philosophy #11: Never have 50/50 partnerships)

It must be clear that one individual will have the final decision and the rest involved will need to trust and accept that decision. It is better to have someone take control versus sitting around waiting for something to happen. Keep in mind, a leader is not born but is created through trial and errors. A good leader will make mistakes at times but will learn from those mistakes.

I went to a boot camp facility where I observed someone breaking their chain of command and failed to listen to the person in charge. The individual's punishment was to wear a string chain fastened by safety pins to their commanding leader for the entire day. This reprimand was to stress the importance of following and setting a chain of command – there must be leaders and there needs to be workers; one queen bee and many pollinators; one chief and many Indians. The reason a 50/50 partnership does not work in many cases is that numerous times I have seen partners get caught up in disagreements where nothing can be agreed upon. When this occurs there is wasted time & energy going back and forth trying to resolve the conflict during which the corporations suffer from the lack of momentum to move forward. Sometimes a stalemate occurs as in the game of chess where neither side wins causing the end result to be splitting the corporation or even complete elimination of the business with two losers.

I typically recommend the one investing the most capital to become the majority stock holder creating a 51% to 44% partnership. This 5% gap is for two reasons: One, it gives a clear picture who is in charge and second, it leaves 5% shares available for future investors or partners to come aboard. The remaining 5% shares can also be used for keeping employees longevity and loyalty to the company by offering non-voting shares. This term is referred to as the 'Golden Handcuffs'.

With Philosophy #11 in mind, who is the President of the corporation?

_____

How many shares of the company will this person possess?_____

The President of the corporation is ultimately responsible for everything. Often the president is also the CEO (Chief Executive Officer) which has the responsibility of ensuring profits to the other partners, shareholders, investors, board of directors, and to the employees. The CEO presides over day to day operations and must be money conscientious with balance and budgeting skills.

The next position in a company ORG chart is the Vice President (VP). The VP is responsible for sales growth, new products, and services. The Executive Secretary is the signer of legal documents and performs the checks and balances. This individual should understand the tasks and responsibilities of the other officers and help them succeed. If your corporation consists of only two people, the VP can assume the Executive Secretary role for the company. One person can hold two or more positions in a corporation. The ORG chart of a company expands greatly as a company grows and a whole new chain of command transpires.

Who is the VP? _____ at _____%

Who is the Secretary?_____ at _____%

    An enterprise corporation may have an ORG chart of executives that would also include the following titles: CFO (Chief Financial Officer), COO (Chief Operations Officer), CIO (Chief Information Officer), CTO (Chief Technology Officer), and others. In addition, a corporation may have:

Controller = Management level position responsible for supervising the quality of accounting and financial reporting to the executives.

Managers = Verifies quality of work being performed by all employees.

Supervisors = Direct employee contact ensuring prosperity of work

Employees = Sales Reps, Fabrication Workers, Assembly Lines, etc.

List other officers of the company and their shares of ownership:

    _____ at _____%

    _____ at _____%

What other positions are available within the company?

_____ _____ _____

Who will fill these positions?

_____ _____ _____

Starting a business does not have to be complicated, it can be completed in a matter of 4 EASY steps:

1. File your business name with Secretary of State

Certificate of Assumed Business Name, Fee is around $25.00

Alabama	www.sos.state.al.us	Nebraska	www.nol.org/home/sos
Alaska	www.commerce.state.ak.us/occ	Nevada	www.sos.state.nv.us
Arizona	www.azsos.gov	New Hampshire	www.sos.nh.gov
Arkansas	www.sos.arkansas.gov	New Jersey	www.state.nj.us/state
California	www.ss.ca.gov	New Mexico	www.sos.state.nm.us
Colorado	www.sos.state.co.us	New York	www.dos.state.ny.us
Connecticut	www.sots.state.ct.us	N. Carolina	www.secstate.state.nc.us
Delaware	www.sos.delaware.gov	N. Dakota	www.nd.gov/sos
Dist. Columbia	www.os.dc.gov	Ohio	www.state.oh.us/sos
Florida	www.dos.state.fl.us	Oklahoma	www.sos.state.ok.us
Georgia	www.sos.state.ga.us	Oregon	www.sos.state.or.us
Hawaii	www.hawaii.gov/dcca/breg	Pennsylvania	www.dos.state.pa.us
Idaho	www.sos.idaho.gov	Rhode Island	www.state.ri.us
Illinois	www.sos.state.il.us	S. Carolina	www.scsos.us
Indiana	www.in.gov/sos	S. Dakota	www.state.sd.us/sos/sos.htm
Iowa	www.sos.state.ia.us	Tennessee	www.tennessee.gov/sos
Kansas	www.kssos.org	Texas	www.sos.state.tx.us
Kentucky	www.sos.ky.gov	Utah	www.utah.gov/services
Louisiana	www.sec.state.la.us	Vermont	www.sec.state.vt.us
Maine	www.state.me.us/sos	Virginia	www.commonwealth.virginia.gov
Maryland	www.sos.state.md.us	Washington	www.secstate.wa.gov
Massachusetts	www.sec.state.ma.us	West Virginia	www.wvsos.com
Michigan	www.michigan.gov/sos	Wisconsin	www.wdfi.org
Minnesota	www.sos.state.mn.us	Wyoming	www.state.wy.us
Mississippi	www.sos.ms.gov	Guam	www.ns.gov.gu
Missouri	www.sos.mo.gov	Puerto Rico	www.estado.gobierno.pr
Montana	www.sos.mt.gov	Virgin Islands	www.ltg.gov.vi

2. Apply for a Federal Tax ID Number (Employer ID)

At IRS website complete the SS-4 EIN Application Form located at:

http://www.irs.gov/pub/irs-pdf/fss4.pdf (FREE)

Further detailed instructions are found at: http://www.irs.gov/pub/irs-pdf/iss4.pdf

3. Obtain your State Sales Tax Permit "Seller's Permit #"

If you are selling any products or services that are subject to sales tax in your state, you must collect tax from customers and pay that money back to the state.

4. Setup a business checking account and obtain any required local licenses/permits.

With these steps completed you are now ready to meet the market demand.

Principle #7: Meet the Demand

You can have the best business concept in the world, but without marketing the chances of success will be limited. Fortunately, in this day of exponential times there are plenty of opportunities to spread the word of your business to the world. We live in a time where "viral marketing" is the key. Viral marketing is like an airborne pathogen moving through the air, this includes foundations such as Facebook, Craigslist, Twitter, and email. This type of medium allows a business to reach out to their customers on a regular basis at a very low expense. These venues listed above are viral marketing methods of delivering a message to consumers. Chapter 7 will answer how the message should <u>appear</u> and <u>who</u> it should be concentrated towards.

(Philosophy #12: A precise and concise marketing plan is mandatory)

The <u>appearance</u> of the message you present needs to be the same for all of your marketing efforts. From the presentation of products on the shelf to your website; they must be positioned and placed correctly. From business cards to brochures; they must appeal to the customer and have uniformity. Each ad must represent a desire to buy; encouraging the consumer to spend their hard earned money on you and your product.

From the name of your business to the color of your logo your sales strategy and marketing plan requires an image that makes the customer feel important, special, and comfortable in order to enhance their shopping experience. List propositions of why the customer needs your product or service. Think outside the box; creativity grabs the attention of consumers so come up with compelling reasons for a shopper to buy. To boost the overall customer experience, consider offering amenities such as coffee, free shipping, gift wrapping, etc. Your marketing image must match or even precede your claim on paper. Whether advertising low prices, high quality of products, or exceptional service, you must live up to the expectations you are setting. Good PR (Public Relations) is essential for businesses to grow. If your business doesn't appeal to consumers they will go elsewhere. The retail store needs to be clean and so does your website. Have a professional appearance; broken links or trash on the floor diminishes credibility. From the opening of your mouth to the first step into your store, everything must look like it was properly thought out and placed specifically for a purpose.

'Target advertising' answers to <u>whom</u> you should be marketing towards. Focus your marketing campaign on specific areas to attract customers that are most likely interested in buying your product. The focal point of your marketing efforts should be set on the consumer which best fits the market research you performed earlier in chapter 4. SRS invested advertising dollars on a website targeted towards computer hardware products at a low price. This website was 100% geared towards our type of clientele and cost $1,000 per month. However, this website returned us $10k per month in profits; it was well worth the dollars invested. Locating the appropriate advertisement venues will save the added cost of hiring additional sales reps.

(Philosophy #13: Never add an employee who doesn't pay for themselves)

Each new customer is an advocate in helping spread the word of your business. If their experience was pleasant, it is believed they will tell three others about their encounter; keep in mind, they will tell ten more if they feel dissatisfied. It is important to build relationships with each customer, reminding them to pick you above the competition. Begin collecting data on each customer including phone numbers, addresses, and especially email addresses. Use this information for sending promotional offers, newsletters, and thank you cards for supporting your business. At Computer Central a customer's phone number is used as their account number. By tracking purchases in this manner, it's convenient and gives an opportunity to call customers regarding new products or special offers.

Throughout twelve years of business a vast amount of advertising dollars passed through the corporation. Since 2010 my favorite means of advertising has been '**viral marketing**'. I simply post, and receive instant feedback. I placed an ad on our Facebook fan page stating, the first 5 buyers would receive a free shirt, within 10 minutes our first item sold! Thirty minutes later each item was gone. Thousands of dollars could have been spent on radio, TV, or other media and never receive that type of a reaction or success...not to mention, it was free advertising.

In 1999 there was a business which had a clever idea to create a fishing pole holder that lit up when a fish bit the bait. The company was convinced their product would sell to the masses and hired us to develop a website for them. After spending $5k for a website with flash media content and a full featured description of their product, the sales did not come rolling in as expected. The problem was not the product, but rather, not knowing how to deliver their message to the consumer.

I can't stress how important it is to create free viral marketing advocates ASAP! I have placed ads on each and received a positive experience. My mother, Vickie often stated, "All it takes to become a millionaire is to sell something at a dollar profit a million times". It used to be difficult to spread the word to a million potential buyers, however, times have changed. The way to reach the masses is via the internet. It took the radio 38 years to reach a market audience of 50 million people, the TV took 13 years and the internet only 4. Facebook however, reached 50 million people in just 2 years. The amount of internet devices connecting to the web today is well over a billion, making it exceptionally easy to reach out to millions of potential customers and you becoming a millionaire.

A kid in the UK needed money for college and created the website www.milliondollarhomepage.com. He began selling pixels for $1.00 each and soon, he had sold a million. The outcome is a prime example of my mother's quote and someone using it to become a millionaire.

(Philosophy #14 Track ROI (return on investment))

For every dollar spent there needs to be a return to the company. ROI (return on investment) is making sure the money spent is worth the investment. For years I spent $5k a month on phonebook ads, now I barely spend $300. Each month on Google alone there are over 31 billion searches while phonebook use is rapidly declining. From advertising budgets to technology advancements – tracking through reporting should clearly show a net profit. Spend time adding your website to free internet advertising sites including Google and other search engines. You need to ensure your place in this medium of viral marketing.

Providing tangible material to customers will build brand awareness. Having logos printed on shirts, pens, flash drives, and other media provides customer loyalty. Consumers wearing a logoed shirt offers free advertisement for the business. T-shirts can be purchased for $3.50 each and pens for much less. These are inexpensive ways of keeping your business name and logo in the public eye.

There are local business activists and community involvement organizations I recommend. Your local Chamber of Commerce, BBB (Better Business Bureau), and in Idaho there is an agency called, "Buy Idaho," encouraging others to buy from local vendors versus elsewhere. Every dollar spent within the local community is equal to $10 dollars spent inside your city. The dollars spent locally creates a circle of money supporting the community and supplying jobs.

Become a consultant versus a salesman. Offer solutions for your customers and not a sale. I encourage you to get involve with lead groups (local business people helping one another develop new contacts), school alumni's, and to talk with the business review for a free write-up about your business. Begin networking with others, promoting your business, and closing deals; the ABC of business (Always Be Closing).

Where will you advertise?_____
_____ _____ _____

How will you promote your business?_____

What is your advertising budget?_____

Do you have brochures?_____ Do they portray the right image? _____

Is it defining, attractive, easy to read, and to the point?_____
(an example can be seen at: www.computercentral.com/brochure)

Do your business cards offer a solution and define your business
accurately?_____ Does your logo fit your business?_____

What is your slogan / tagline? _____
_____
    (Computer Central's is : *"Putting the personal back into personal computers"*)

Do you have a website? _____
    If Yes, what is the URL?_____

Have you created a Facebook fan page for your business?_____
    If yes, What is the link? _____
    http://www.facebook.com

Do you have a Twitter page?_____
    http://twitter.com

Do you have a Linkedin website? ____
    http://www.linkedin.com

List other marketing areas / campaigns you will engage in:
_____
_____
_____
_____

Principle #8: Prepare Attitude and Aptitude

Success is having a satisfactory completion of something or the gaining of wealth either financial or mental. As we go through business adventures we gain a wealth of knowledge improving the way we do things. It won't be easy and there will be bumps along the way, success is knowing failure, yet rising every time you fall. The power to win is in your own hands.

(Philosophy #15: Don't fear opposition –
let the competition fear you.)

My twin brother's favorite quote growing up was, "Rise, go forth, and conquer". Having this type of attitude helps increase your will-power to move forward. Preparing your attitude for business is to realize that the competition can be like a large oil tanker which takes time and room to maneuver, whereas smaller companies can move like a jet-ski in the water, being swift and accurate. Another scenario I use... Alligators may be ferocious but little piranhas can take out a large alligator one nibble at a time. It only takes dedication, determination, and the removal of fear to begin a new journey.

What would you do if you took fear out of the equation?

_____

_____

Too often people say, "I was going to start a business", "I don't have the money to start a business", "If I was only younger", and "I just can't take the risk". These quotes are what keep the majority of people from becoming an entrepreneur. Plato once said, "We can easily forgive a child who is afraid of the dark, the real tragedy is a man who is afraid of the light" – meaning don't be afraid to take the risk to succeed. "You will always be what you have always been and will always do what you have always done". Putting that first step into action typically requires some type of change and doing something different than the normal day to day routine. The definition of insanity is doing the same thing over and over expecting a different result. In order to avoid being insane it requires doing something different in your life.

What changes are required to move forward?_____

_____

What fears do you have? _____

_____

What "self-talk" would help overcome these fears? _____

_____

_____

Aptitude is like Michael Jordon's natural ability of accomplishing something at a much easier scope than others. My daughter Kaylin is a natural entrepreneur and began working on her PC at the age of 4 absorbing the education of technology very quickly. My wife and I tried one day to illustrate to our two daughters how important money is and told them that we need to start saving more or we will run out. Kaylin at age 8 became worried and was determined to find work. Unannounced to my wife and I, Kaylin began surfing Google for jobs. Although jobs for an eight year old are in short supply, she none the less brought us a list of jobs she could do to help make and save money….that's aptitude!

One who can hear, speak, do, and then teach others is an individual who proves they are capable of being an entrepreneur. They learn from the past, live for the present, and create the future by challenging themselves daily and setting goals to ensure they are on target for success. This doesn't mean mistakes are not made, but it does mean learning from those mistakes and rising to the occasion.

So what if you're not born with an aptitude where a special trait comes naturally? I know my limits and could never be an artist or a singer; I don't have the aptitude for either of those traits. However, people can accomplish their dreams, it just requires more education and hard work. Education consists of many avenues including college to trade schools. This reminds me of a quote, "Don't let schooling interfere with your education". There are many ways to become educated and sometimes the easiest is being self-taught. I went to college for four years, the majority of my education in computers was through certifications and experiences. Look into certs, trade schools, or other training facilities to save money.

Is there additional training or certifications you can obtain to help succeed in business? _____

_____

What are your daily goals?_____

_____

_____

_____

What new challenges are you ready to take on?_____

_____

_____

Bankers, VC's (Venture Capitalist), or potential investors are investing their money and trust in you, not necessarily the idea you are selling. They want to know you are well trained and adverse in your industry. These people are truly investing in your performance, your motivational drive, and determination of success. Your confidence of achievement influences others to be on board with you. It is important for investors and customers to feel confident in you and have no doubt in your skills or ability to deliver. Stop and imagine the success you want and then expect it.

What success do you want to achieve? _____

_____

_____

How will you convince others? _____

You may wonder why some businesses do better than others. The most important reason is leadership. A successful entrepreneur must be able to lead. They need to lead co-workers, customers, associates, and themselves to the visions they clearly and passionately dream about. Your attitude is what sanctions your employees to do well or poor. Being upbeat, positive, joyful, charismatic, and passionate about your business will rub off on others.

What experiences have you had with leadership?_____

_____

What did you learn from these experiences?_____

_____

Which traits are your strongest?_____

_____

Customers often commented how they loved the atmosphere that was radiating as we ran around the store with excitement and eagerness to help. Being passionate about the business leads to a greater success.

Customers are #1, employees are #2, and you are #3 when it comes to being the owner. Customers are number one because without them there is no revenue, employees are number two because they are dynamic (I have spent thousands training employees from being good to becoming excellent at what they do...just to have them leave and compete against me), Owners are number three because the best leader is one who assists their employees in achieving goals. Customers are essential, but those customers won't buy if your employees are not feeling and doing their best. Encouraging employees on their strengths versus weaknesses will help boost morale. The overall outcome is ensuring customers have the utmost positive buying experience.

What things are you passionate about in the business?

_____

_____

Is there anyway of creating a more exciting atmosphere?

_____

_____

_____

What will customers say about your business?

_____

_____

_____

What are your aptitudes (things you are naturally good at)?_____

_____

_____

Principle #9: Focus on Efficiency

(Philosophy #16: Inefficiency is a waste of money)

The goal for efficiency is to create a business that runs smoothly and effortlessly…like a well-oiled machine. In order to achieve efficiency there are three topics to concentrate on: **Time**, **Performance**, & **Inventory**.

Minimizing the actions required to perform a task will save "Time". Time does equal money, especially to the employer who is paying for unproductiveness. Don't allow unproductive employees to cost more than they earn the company. When employees work too slowly it is a waste of resources, when they work too quickly it cost time and money for fixing mistakes. Trying to find that fine balance of productivity versus quality performance is the magic recipe. "Meissen," a culinary term, illustrates the art of efficiency by having all ingredients readily available to prevent wasted time – less movement saves time.

(Philosophy #17: Let technology replace unproductive manpower).

Nearly every week I find cost savings for businesses. Some of the recent changes in technology makes for huge savings. Simply changing antiquated analog phone lines at $36.99 a piece to SIP (Session Initiation Protocol) trunks at $10 per line saves $100's per month. In addition, changing fax lines to electronic faxing services saves another $20 per month. These savings also come with added benefits and features that save money. With digital faxes the inefficiency of people walking to and from a fax machine goes away. Each fax is sent and received via email saving costs on paper and toner. Changing to an updated phone system makes for ease of use and quicker responses. Voicemails are sent as a sound file to an email that can easily be played through any smart phone. Technology is amazing and is an essential part of making a business efficient.

(Philosophy #18: Evaluate strategies often)

Evaluating strategies often is an important step for businesses to attain the highest level of proficiency. For every dollar saved is one less sell one may have to make. Review credit card fees, interest rates, and other costly items where you might be able to do better. Discover new ways to help each person be as useful as possible. The least amount of movement required to complete a task saves countless time and money.

(Philosophy #19: Every step entails a price)

Large corporations have performed studies putting a price on each step taken within their corporation…the results are quite surprising. Consider someone making $40/hour who visits the bathroom twice a day, takes a break, gets something to drink, and stands around talking to other employees. Those small tasks add up, before you know it you just paid out $40+ dollars for an hour of trivial unproductive tasks. In addition, the hourly wage you think you're paying…is quite a bit more.

According to Microsoft's Invoice Template & Profit Calculator you are actually paying $53.29/hour after just the basic employment taxes and other fees. This price does not include their use of the electricity, office space, computer equipment, and other necessary expenses they accrue. Even an employee receiving only $7.50/hour, their true hourly wage for the company is $9.94/hour, including a zero benefit package. That extra $2.44/hour goes to state and federal taxes which include: FICA, FUTA, and Medicare.

FICA = Federal Insurance Contributions Act where 12.4% of earned income must be paid into Social Security, and an additional 2.9% must be paid into Medicare
FUTA = The Federal Unemployment Tax Act is money taken to provide payments for unemployment compensation to workers who have lost their jobs.
Medicare = A social insurance program administered by the United States government, providing health insurance coverage to people age 65 or disabled.

The more you keep employees working at their desks, on an assembly line, or in their work station is extra money saved for the company. To sum up the objective for achieving efficiency, "Time" is determined by the costs of an employee and discovering ways to minimize movements required to perform those tasks.

The second topic of efficiency is "Performance" where getting the most out of an employee saves money. I often share with people, my employees wear multiple hats, working as a team for the corporation.

(Philosophy #20: Wearing multiple hats saves money and space)

If the phone rings and the sales reps are busy, other team members will quickly answer the phone to assist the customer. Most corporations can consolidate one, two, or even three employees by doing simple cross-training. Educating employees to be competent in other areas of the business saves money. The phone receptionist can call on account receivables (money owed to the company) and the bookkeeper can help direct calls. I recall an order of 500 computers having a deadline to ship by the end of the week. Every employee assisted in making it come to fruition. Employees who never assembled a computer before, were unboxing chassis and assisting in other areas. This camaraderie and team playing environment builds loyalty and involves everyone. As the CEO of SR-Systems Inc., I ensure profits to my shareholders and also do the purchasing, and maintained my own clientele. This kept me in a healthy competition with my sales force. By performing the purchasing I could keep the cost low and an eye on inventory costs.

Inventory is the final topic we'll discuss in this chapter. I am reminded of a quote by Dr. Deming, "There is very little work in anything; provided you eliminate the waste". "JIT" is a term used in manufacturing facilities which stands for Just-In-Time inventory. Not too much and not too little is the goal when it comes to inventory. It is ineffective to have way too much of anything whether it is people, utensils, or product inventory. Most material can be delivered within just a couple of days and there is no reason to have a surplus of inventory. In the computer industry, inventory is a huge cost and must be sold quickly before newer products are released. I calculated the majority of computer hardware components have a shelf-life of 45 days. A revolving door of inventory being sold and replenished in a timely fashion prevents products from becoming obsolete. You must remember, inventory = Money. More importantly, it is cash taken from your operating capital that could be used for other things. Businesses have gone under due to a surplus of inventory. In the restaurant business the food can only last so long before spoilage occurs. It is a tough balance one must juggle and watch cautiously in order to prevent an over-abundance or an insufficient amount of inventory to conduct business.

The topics we've discussed in chapter 9 "Focusing on Efficiency" entails: Time, Performance, & Inventory. These are the top priorities to focus upon and then begin searching other methods to protect your money. If you're not watching the bottom dollar money can leak out, before you know it, there is no money left. I hate wasted time – but more importantly, I hate wasted money. The only way to know why, where, and how your money is being spent is through reporting which leads us to chapter 10.

Are there inefficiencies in your business that can be fixed?

_____
_____
_____
_____
_____

Can you locate technology to replace inefficiencies?

_____
_____
_____
_____
_____

Are there job functions that can be consolidated?

_____
_____
_____
_____
_____

Principle #10: Implement Reporting

This chapter illustrates the two most important reports that every business owner or manager must know.

(Philosophy #21: Reporting is vital to maximize profits)

The first report to carefully monitor is the P&L (**Profit & Loss**) income statement. This report shows the money coming in and the amount of money going out. The end result of a P&L is the net profit produced. Here's an example of a P&L Statement:

Profit & Loss
January 1 – December 31st, 2012

Ordinary Income/Expense		*Defined*
Income		
4010 · Products Sold	50,000.00	
4050 · Service Work	10,000.00	Sales Generated
Total · SALES REVEUNE	$60,000.00	
Expenses		
5020 · Material (COGS)	30,000.00	
5010 · Freight Expense	500.00	Cost of Inventory
Total · Cost of Goods Sold	$30,500.00	
Net Ordinary Income (Gross Profit)	**$29,500.00**	= Sales - Cost
Other Expenses		
6000 · LABOR		
6105 · Sales Reps	10,000.00	
6106 · Service Reps	5,000.00	
6100 · Advertising	250.00	
6200 · Merchant Billing & Fees	1,500.00	All Expenses
6300 · Repairs & Maintenance	50.00	
6400 · Rent	1,000.00	
6500 · Utilities	500.00	
Total Expense	18,300.00	
Net Income	**$11,200.00**	Actual Profit

The first section of this report illustrates the sales produced. Each month one must generate reports to review the profits or negatives created. Separating each revenue source by department will make for better tracking and allow for quicker review.

What is your estimated sales per month? $_____/month

What departments will you have in your business? 1._____
2._____ 3._____ 4._____

How much revenue (sales) will each department produce?
1.$_____/month 2.$_____/month 3.$_____/month 4.$_____/month

The next entry is the COGS (Cost of Goods Sold). COGS convey the amount of money spent for the products sold.

What is the estimated COGS for each month? $_____/month
(ie: If a restaurant business sells a hamburger for $5.00 the COGS would equal all the costs involved to make that hamburger. These costs include the bun, meat, onion, lettuce, tomato, ketchup, & mustard. When adding all these ingredients, the total may equal $4.00... that number is the COGS.)

Subtracting the sales made (top dollar amount) from the COGS (the second dollar amount) equals Gross Profit.

What is the estimated monthly Gross Profit? $_____/month
(Sales per month – COGS)

The third section on a P&L are the other expenses it took to operate a business. These expenses include payroll, rent, utilities, advertising, insurance, janitorial, office supplies, shipping, credit card fees, legal & professional expenses.

Credit card fees are called 'Merchant Services' which is the percent taken by the credit card company for allowing the acceptance of credit cards. These fees start at a .25 cent charge plus a 3.5% transaction fee. On a $10.00 item .60 cents (3.5% + .25 cents) can be deducted from your profits just by accepting a credit card. These merchant fees accumulate to over $80k / year within SRS. Credit card fees are a definite number that one must factor when calculating expenses for a business.

What are the estimated monthly Expenses for each item?

Payroll	$_____/month	Janitorial	$_____/month
Rent	$_____/month	Shipping	$_____/month
Utilities	$_____/month	Merchant Fees	$_____/month
Advertising	$_____/month	Office Supplies	$_____/month
Insurance	$_____/month	Legal Fees	$_____/month

What are the total monthly expenses for these items? $_____/month
Are there other expenses that should be listed? $_____/month
If so, what is the new total monthly expenses? $_____/month

The Final item is your "NET Profit" which is the difference between your Gross Profit and Total Expenses.

What is your estimated Net Profit (Gross Profit – Total Expenses)?

$_____/month

What percent increase do you anticipate each year? _____%
    (on average expect a growth rate of at least 5% per year)

What is the estimated Net Profit in 5 years? $_____

Does this number justify having a business and make you feel content in the business's potential profits? _____.

Are there changes that can be made in sales or in the expenses?_____.
What changes can be done? _____

_____

How do these changes affect the business? _____

_____

How much savings can these changes produce? $_____/month

A 5% increase in sales or a 5% reduction in costs makes an enormous difference. For businesses generating $10k per month in sales and discovers a reduction of 5% in the cost of goods sold, will increase profits $500 per month! Furthermore, if one can increase sales by 5% then a total of $1,000 per month will be generated.

The next report for entrepreneurs is the **balance sheet**. The balance sheet illustrates the finances of a company by listing the amount of <u>money</u>, <u>inventory</u>, and <u>A/R</u> (account receivables) a company possesses. These three items are called 'current assets', belongings that can be turned into cash in a reasonable amount of time, "Liquid Assets".

ASSETS
  Current Assets
    Checking/Savings

1110 · **Checking**	50,000.00	
1120 · **Savings**	10,500.00	
1130 · **Petty Cash**	200.00	
Total Checking/Savings	60,700.00	
Account Receivables	5,000.00	
Inventory	10,000.00	
Total Current Assets	75,700.00	

What is the balance in the company checking account? $_____
Savings? $_____ Stocks? $_____ Other? $_____

How much money do you have in inventory? $_____ A/R $_____

What is the Total of these Current Assets? $_____ (everything added)

The second section is your 'fixed assets' which include: vehicles, office equipment (computers, servers, phone systems, tools, etc.) and furniture (chairs, desks, shelving, displays, etc.). These amenities can be turned into cash if sold, but takes longer to obtain. Fixed assets are usually sold at a depreciated amount becoming less valuable over time. An example of a balance sheet's fixed assets report is similar to this:

Fixed Assets

1501 · Furniture & Equipment	35,000	
1510 · Office Equipment	15,000	
1530 · Automobiles	50,000	

Total Fixed Assets   100,000

TOTAL ASSETS $175,700 = (Fixed Assets + Current Assets)

Does the company own any vehicles?_____. If yes, list the value: $_____

How much money does the company have in equipment? $_____

How much money does the company have in furniture/fixtures? $_____

What is the Total of these Fixed Assets? $_____

What is the Total of Current Assets + Fixed Assets? $_____
                              (This number equals your Total Assets)

The next section of a Balance Sheet lists debts, known as "Liabilities". The liabilities of a company include the amount of money owed to vendors, credit cards, loans, etc. and would like similar to this:

LIABILITIES & EQUITY
    Current Liabilities

2000 · Accounts Payable	78,304.17	(money owed to vendors / suppliers)
2015 · Credit Cards	1,500.00	(company purchases on credit card)
2140 · Payroll Liabilities	2,000.00	(payroll taxes)
2400 · Loans	4,000.00	(money borrowed to begin business)
2500 · Bank Line of Credit	5,000.00	(LOC from a financial institute)

==============

    TOTAL ASSETS   **$175,700**

Is there money owed to vendors?_____ (yes/no)
    If Yes, How much? $_____

Does the company owe money on credit cards?_____ (yes/no)
    If Yes, how much? $_____

Does the company have any loans?_____ (yes/no)
    If Yes, how much? $_____

Are there any other liabilities / debts the company has?_____(yes/no)
    If Yes, how much? $_____

What is the total amount of Liabilities owed? $_____

What is your total Liabilities & Equities? $_____

Keeping an eye on each of these reports will prevent financial surprises. Review these reports every two weeks while looking for possibilities to maximize profits.

Principle #11: Ensure Appropriate Financing

In this chapter we'll discuss monetary flow. To begin, there are five ways of obtaining money:

1. You can heist or steal it
2. You can be fortunate and inherit it
3. You can be lucky and find it
4. You can be fortuitous and win it
5. Or most importantly – you can earn it!

Earning money is the focus throughout this book. I say to my wife – "I work way too hard for you to buy a lottery ticket and win – it takes away from the work I do and the challenge of earning it." Being creative and having that drive towards success keeps life interesting.

Once you have money there are only three ways to keep it:

1. Save
2. Invest
3. Spend less

In business there are only three ways to increase your profits:

1. Create more sales
2. Lower expenditures
3. Successfully re-invest it

A successful business owner whose eye is always on the bottom line will do all three. It's imperative to focus on selling more, keeping expenses low, and investing wisely.

The monetary flow is how money comes in and how it goes out. An entrepreneur's first dollar spent usually comes from their own pocket. That dollar is used for various setup costs, which may have included this book. Money is then spent on inventory which is sold for a profit to consumers. The profit earned will increase your bank account, so you can buy more products and pay for the overhead of running a business. It is essential to keep the amount of money coming in higher than what is going out. In order to ensure lucrativeness we need to create a budget analysis.

A _budget analysis_ provides a comprehensive assessment of expenditures to identify potential areas to save costs. These next series of questions will help build the P&L and balance sheet. The cash flow projections on paper must show profitability or there is no sense in continuing without drastic changes to your financial plan. Let's see how your business idea pans out:

How much capital (money) will you open the business with?
$_____

What is the estimated monthly rent for the business?
$_____

Will employees be hired? _____ If yes, how many? _____

How much will the average employee get paid per hour? _____

How much do you anticipate for monthly utilities?_____
(water, sewer, trash, phone, insurance, power, gas, internet, etc.)

How much will licenses and permits cost? _____

Do you have an emergency fund? _____ If Yes, How much? $_____
          (be aware of unforeseen circumstances)

Will there be enough profit for a successful business venture? _____

A term I like to caution people about is, "habit spending". This phrase I use for unnecessary items people buy on a regular basis. These purchases could be as insignificant as a daily routine of buying coffee, soda, snacks, cigarettes, lottery tickets, lunches, etc. These are examples that take away from cash and slowly cut away the budget. Personally, I had a daily "habit spending" of buying coffee. One day I calculated the amount of money I was spending each year and it totaled around $2,000. With that realization, I decided to cut my coffee intake and began brewing coffee at home.

The point is – spend and think wisely – If you have a "habit spending" in your personal life, it is easy to incorporate them into your business. The last thing a business needs is a credit card with interest at 20% where making the minimum payment never pays off the original purchase. Credit (using someone else's money to pay for things) is required at times, but it must make good business sense before doing so. I use my American Express card on a regular basis for company purchases in order to rack up reward points. Currently I have over a million reward points where I can travel around the World for free. However, each time I use my Amex card I make sure it is paid in full at the end of every month. Recognizing needs versus wants - helps in prudent spending.

(Philosophy #22: If business is not innovating it could be dying)

Be creative in your spending and find ways to limit your expenditures. Locate ways to cut costs, to seek out new opportunities, and to accelerate your growth. The latest trend is Energy Conservation. A recent investment, "Enhanced Power Technologies," focuses on power savings. They have saved schools and businesses money just by making small modifications to energy equipment. Even by shutting off lights, computers, fans, HVAC units, and other power using devices will save money.

A phrase I mentioned at the beginning of this book, "soft costs," are out of sight expenses a business pays in order to reach a sale. These expenditures are not easily identifiable and often overlooked. Moreover, they can be difficult to calculate which creates a challenging issue when trying to factor them in. The best way to describe "soft costs" is by calling them the "phantoms" around the office.

These phantoms are the missing and used pens, pencils, paper, ink, toners, tape, staples, shipping material, cleaning supplies, paper towels, paper cups, toilet paper, and the list goes on and on. These items simply vanish quickly and certainly add up over time. Many of these items are required to conduct transactions and are found where people congregate or spend any amount of time. "Soft costs" are necessities used every day – nevertheless their effect on the balance sheet are permanent and palpable.

A way to account for these soft costs is by applying a 5% padding to every item sold. For example, if an item cost $10.00, add 5% to the cost making the "new cost" $10.50. In a sales commission position it allows for sales reps to know the cost of doing business; they are aware that no commission is paid out unless the sale is above the 5% pad. Soft costs are a definite expense and must be factored when performing a sell. This padding also helps pay for the valuable employees who don't generate profits, but who are equally essential to the function of the business: warehouse workers, drivers, secretaries, accounting department, etc. We could just as well call them overhead.

Overhead is like a giant monster that must be fed, if you don't feed it, it will consume your business. From the lease of a building, utilities, office supplies, and the marketing; overhead is all the expenses it takes to run a business. The largest overhead is typically the employees – from their wages to their incentives, including bonuses, insurance, 401k, per diem, training, etc.

The topics discussed in this chapter: soft costs, expenditures, and overhead have to do with the flow of money. The goal is to keep more money coming in than what is going out. Watching every dollar spent is how to secure a positive exit strategy.

What are some "soft costs" you need to consider? _____
_____
_____

How can you save costs? _____
_____
_____

What is your largest overhead? _____
    How much will it cost you per month? $_____

List your expenditures: _____
_____

Have you considered fuel costs, packaging, etc.? _____

What is the total expenditures per month? $_____

Do you personally have any credit cards? _____
If Yes, What are they: _____ Current Balance $_____
What is the interest rate? _____% (try shopping for a lower rate)

What is the plan to pay off this credit card? _____
_____
_____
_____

Will you need to borrow money to begin this business adventure? _____
If yes, How much money will be required? $_____

PRINCIPLE #12: PLAN AN EXIT STRATEGY

The term "exit" relates to having a plan for a business owner to walk away. For some, it will be forced upon them due to bad management, changes in the economy, or disasters. For others it will be planned through retirement or sale of the business. For all who are playing it safe; know there are no guarantees in business. Instead, educate yourself and plan to buy, build, and sell.

(Philosophy #23 Written processes & procedures provide rest for the future)

With buy, build, and sell in mind, one should set goals to accomplish for the future. It is necessary for a business to function without constant presence. To accomplish this, one must have a good system of written procedures for day to day operations. Begin writing these procedures now to make life easier for the future. If you have a POS (Point of Sale) database write out the process of adding a new product or SKU (stock-keeping unit). Purchase a three ring binder and label it "Operation Manual", then continue adding as new processes arrive.

McDonalds is a great example of a corporation that has written procedures for everything. If an employee doesn't know how to perform a particular job function – they simply look in their operation manual.

Once a clear operation manual is written, it is easy to present a qualified business image to others. Take the information gathered from this workbook to a financial institute to buy a business, expand your business, or to sell the business model to others.

(Philosophy #24: The power of persistence is priceless)

Be a prospector in business, searching for fine gold dust to save money through-out the company. Each department has the opportunity of doing their share of conservation and advancement. There comes a point in every business where the peak performance is reached. The choice comes to either locate other investors, expand, or to sell. A reason to sell is the cost of expanding is expensive and a VC (venture capitalist) could run it better with more money. Don't fall in love with the business – the goal is to buy, build, and then sell so you can be free to spend more time to invest into something new. Be proud of your accomplishments and don't focus on goals you didn't quite reach. Reflect on the mistakes made in the past, but use them to fix the future. Many people spin their wheels in circles expecting a different result which never comes. If you are not getting anywhere in your present situation…it is time for change. This does not mean it is time to give up, it is simply time to seek the opportunities of doing better. Build on your positive strengths and always seek ways of **doing better**.

What is your ultimate goal for opening the business? _____

_____

How will you accomplish this goal?_____

_____

What are some procedures you need to put into place? _____

_____

What systems and processes do you need to write? _____

_____

_____

In closing, I sincerely hope the goal of educating and informing you on the necessities of business was met; while keeping you entertained and interested on the PS 12/24 Principles & Philosophies of business. I value your feedback and invite you to visit www.ps1224.com for updated material, business strategies, and most importantly, for you to begin your **free** online interactive web-based business plan.

I wish you the best success in your business adventures!

Sincerely,

Phil Sigler
P S 12/24

12 Principles to create a business &

24 Philosophies to operate a business

IF YOU CAN'T BE FIRST... YOU MUST BE BETTER!

ABOUT THE AUTHOR

Phil Sigler is the current CEO for SR-Systems Incorporated, Computer Central, SigLaw LLC, and Energy Central. With continued investments and entrepreneurial skills he hopes to educate others through life experiences of running and operating businesses.

www.ingramcontent.com/pod-product-compliance
Lightning Source LLC
Chambersburg PA
CBHW071120210326
41519CB00020B/6359